STEM **trailblaz**

D0607755

SPACE ENGINEER AND SCIENTIST
MARGARET HAMILTON

DOMENICA DI PIAZZA

Lerner Publications • Minneapolis

To Sarah for encouraging me, and to my father for helping with all that math and science homework. And to Margaret Hamilton, for leading the way.

Lerner Publications Company
A division of Lerner Publishing Group, Inc.
241 First Avenue North
Minneapolis, MN 55401 USA

For reading levels and more information, look up this title at www.lernerbooks.com.

Library of Congress Cataloging-in-Publication Data

Names: Di Piazza, Domenica.
Title: Space engineer and scientist Margaret Hamilton / Domenica Di Piazza.
Description: Minneapolis : Lerner Publications, [2018] | Series: STEM trailblazer bios | Audience: Age 7–11. | Audience: Grade 4 to 6. | Includes bibliographical references and index.
Identifiers: LCCN 2016048884 (print) | LCCN 2016050342 (ebook) | ISBN 9781512434507 (lb : alk. paper) | ISBN 9781512456318 (pb : alk. paper) | ISBN 9781512451023 (eb pdf)
Subjects: LCSH: Hamilton, Margaret Heafield, 1936—Juvenile literature. | Project Apollo (U.S.)—History—Juvenile literature. | Computer software developers—United States—Biography—Juvenile literature. | Computer programmers—United States—Biography—Juvenile literature. | Women scientists—United States--Biography—Juvenile literature. | Scientists—United States—Biography—Juvenile literature. | Moon—Juvenile literature.
Classification: LCC QA76.2.H36 D5 2018 (print) | LCC QA76.2.H36 (ebook) | DDC 629.45/4—dc23

LC record available at https://lccn.loc.gov/2016048884

Manufactured in the United States of America
1-42099-25393-3/3/2017

The images in this book are used with the permission of: NASA, pp. 4, 5, 18, 24; Courtesy of Margaret Hamilton, pp. 7, 10, 16, 20; © Wangkun Jia/Dreamstime.com, p. 8; © New York Public Library/Getty Images, p. 11; The Charles Stark Draper Laboratory, Inc. via Smithsonian National Air and Space Museum, NASM2015-06488, p. 12; courtesy of MIT Museum, p. 13; INTERFOTO/Alamy Stock Photo, p. 14; photo by Ray Wallman, courtesy of Margaret Hamilton, p. 19; © Photo12/Universal Images Group/Getty Images, p. 22; © Nicholas Kamm/AFP/Getty Images, p. 26.

Cover: courtesy of MIT Museum.

Main body text set in Adrianna Regular 13/22. Typeface provided by Chank.

CONTENTS

Chapter 1

Buzz Aldrin walks on the surface of the moon.

DOING IT RIGHT

It's July 20, 1969, 10:56 p.m. eastern daylight time. About five hundred million television viewers are glued to their sets. They are watching US astronaut and Apollo 11 mission commander Neil Armstrong step onto the moon. He is the first person in history to walk on the moon. Astronaut Edwin "Buzz" Aldrin joins him twenty minutes later. They plant a US flag on the moon's surface and gather samples of rock. It took a woman to get them there!

EMERGENCY!

But the mission might have failed. Earlier that night, the lunar lander *Eagle* had been scheduled to set down on the moon. Suddenly, the flight software sent flashing warnings. The system was overloaded with jobs to be done. Tension in the

Mission headquarters stayed in contact with the *Apollo 11* astronauts during their lunar landing.

spacecraft and at mission headquarters in Houston, Texas, rose. Would the National Aeronautics and Space Administration (NASA) team have to end the mission? Would the dream of landing on the moon be postponed?

TO THE RESCUE

Back on Earth, thirty-two-year-old **software engineer** Margaret Hamilton held her breath. She had programmed the *Apollo 11* software to spot errors and do its most important jobs first. She hoped it would focus only on landing *Eagle*.

The lander had only thirty seconds of fuel left. Armstrong radioed NASA headquarters: "The *Eagle* has landed." Hamilton's software had done it right. The United States had become the first nation to land humans on the moon.

TECH TALK

"I remember thinking, *Oh my God, it worked*. . . . I was so happy. But I was more happy about [the software] working than about the fact that we landed [on the moon]."

—Margaret Hamilton

MIDWESTERN ROOTS

Margaret H. Heafield was born on August 17, 1936, in Paoli, a small town in southern Indiana. Her father, Kenneth Heafield, was a poet and college professor of philosophy. Her mother, Ruth Esther Heafield, taught high school.

Margaret loved math and science. She liked figuring out how to do things on her own. She wanted to know how the world worked and what motivated people.

Margaret graduated from Hancock High School in 1954. Then she studied math and philosophy at Earlham College in Richmond, Indiana. One of her favorite teachers was Florence Long, the head of the math department. Hamilton wanted to have a career like Long's. She had no idea that the US space program would change her life forever.

In high school, Margaret also liked music, acting, and other arts.

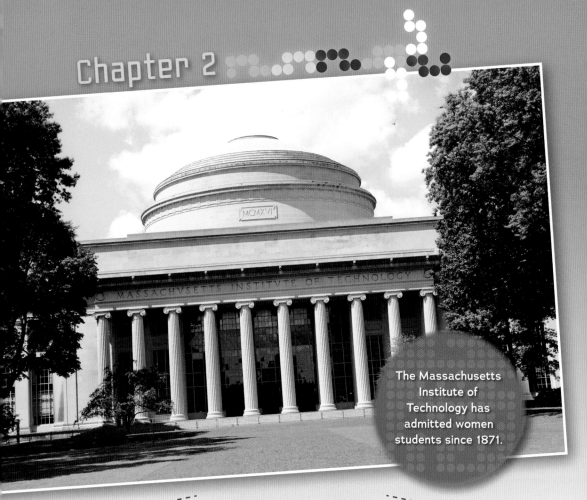

Chapter 2

The Massachusetts Institute of Technology has admitted women students since 1871.

PART OF A TEAM

Hamilton met chemist James Cox Hamilton at Earlham College. The couple married in the late 1950s and moved to Cambridge, Massachusetts, where he studied law at Harvard University. Their daughter, Lauren, was born in 1959.

To support her family, Hamilton accepted a job at the Massachusetts Institute of Technology (MIT) in 1959. She would write software for predicting the weather. The next year, she began working on the Semi-Automatic Ground Environment (SAGE) program at MIT. SAGE developed radar and computer systems for the military to find and track enemy aircraft. The systems also guided weapons to destroy them. Hamilton's job was to program (create software for) SAGE radar systems.

Hamilton was very good at finding—and fixing—errors as she created software. And she fixed them before the programs went live. Hamilton and her coworkers found many mistakes during final testing. They found that most mistakes could be predicted. So she developed software to avoid these errors.

Hamilton loved the exciting new field of computer technology. Computers at that time were huge. They filled

TECH TALK

"From day one, it's been a fascination [for me]—the subject of errors."

—*Margaret Hamilton*

Hamilton was one of the few women who worked in computer technology. But her coworkers respected her.

many rooms. She liked her coworkers. She laughed at their science jokes. She brought Lauren to the lab. Hamilton also worked evenings and weekends there. Very few women worked in computer technology at the time. But she felt that she was part of a team.

THE SPACE RACE

The United States and the Soviet Union were competing to explore space. By the spring of 1961, Soviet astronaut Yuri

Gagarin had become the first person to go into space. He orbited Earth once. Shortly after, US astronaut Alan Shepard flew into space too.

The United States wanted to be the first nation to land a human on the moon. MIT's Charles Stark Draper Laboratory (CSDL) would work with NASA. The team would create the computer programs to guide spacecraft to and from the moon.

Yuri Gagarin spent 108 minutes in space on April 12, 1961.

Chapter 3

Hamilton was part of the Software Engineering Division at Draper Lab.

NOT MAGIC

Hamilton's success at SAGE caught the attention of the Draper Lab. The lab hired her to help write computer code for the Apollo missions.

Computer science was new. Students couldn't take courses

to learn to write code and develop software. So Hamilton and her coworkers experimented. They learned on the job.

In 1965, Hamilton became the director of her team at the lab. Their job was to create software for the mission's two portable computers. One would be on board the *Apollo 11* spacecraft. That craft would take the astronauts and the lander *Eagle* to the moon. The other computer would be on board the *Eagle*. The computers would guide the spacecraft and help land *Eagle* on the moon. Each computer weighed 70 pounds (32 kilograms)!

An engineer works on a computer for the Apollo 11 mission.

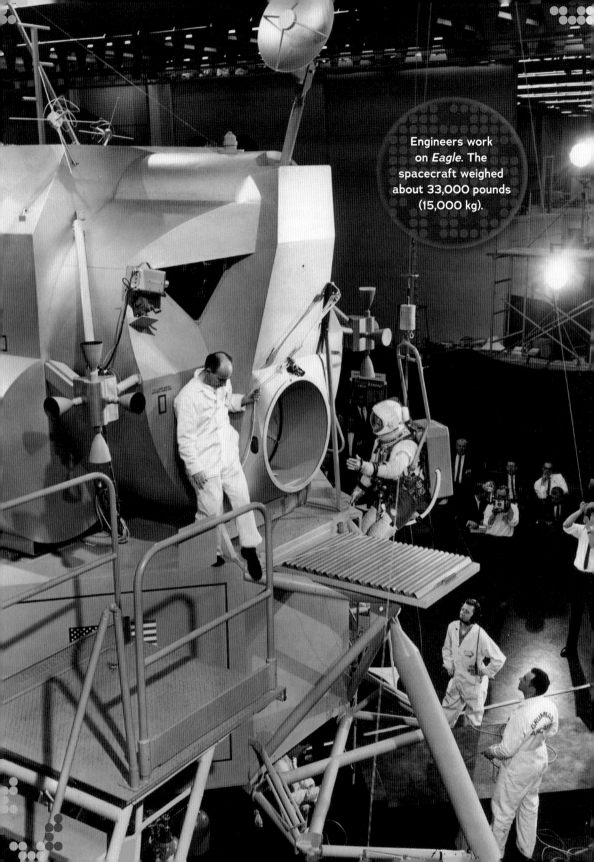

Engineers work on *Eagle*. The spacecraft weighed about 33,000 pounds (15,000 kg).

TECH TALK

At MIT, Hamilton and her coworkers were inventing brand-new ideas in software. "Nobody knew what it was we were doing. It was like the Wild West," she said.

Hamilton knew that reliable software had to prevent mistakes. She and her team skillfully tested the flight hardware and software. She realized that most errors could be avoided— ahead of time.

Hamilton also wanted software to be prepared for the unknown. It should allow an important step to interrupt a less important step. It had to work in real time. It had to know when to override a command. And most important, it had to handle the most pressing jobs first. It had to avoid as many errors as possible.

DOING IT BY HAND

Hamilton's team of software engineers wrote the Apollo Guidance Computer (AGC) code. They used pens or pencils. They wrote it on AGC coding sheets. Then they sent all the

Hamilton's team produced page after page of code. They turned the code into printouts such as this one.

coding sheets to keypunchers. They used keypunch machines to type the code, and the machines cut holes into paper cards. The cards were used to make paper printouts of the code.

At night, a giant computer processed the code. It tested how the code would work on *Eagle*. If problems came up, the team fixed them.

After the code was approved, a group of people went to work. They followed the code, threading copper wires through magnetic rings. They were building the circuit boards, or memory, for the Apollo mission computers.

ART AND MAGIC

Hamilton knew her work was important. But she saw that many people did not think computer **programming** was science. She said that many people thought of it as art and magic. Hamilton used the words *software engineering* to describe her job. It showed that her work was just as scientific as any other engineering. Eventually, the words caught on. Software engineering is considered science. It is not magic.

JULY 20, 1969

By 1969, NASA was ready for the *Apollo 11* takeoff. On July 16, the spacecraft launched from Cape Kennedy (now Cape Canaveral) in Florida. Neil Armstrong, Michael Collins, and Buzz Aldrin were on board. Four days later, more than five hundred million people were glued to their TVs to watch the lunar landing. No one watching in their homes knew that just three minutes before *Eagle* landed, its computers were in trouble. Would the software work? Could it ignore the flood of error messages?

Apollo 11 launches with a three-person crew on July 16, 1969.

Hamilton analyzes data coming in from NASA mission headquarters in Houston.

Hamilton's software saved the mission. The computer focused only on the landing. Armstrong stepped onto the moon. He declared, "[This is] one small step for a man, one giant leap for mankind."

Chapter 4

At HTI, Hamilton worked to make software more reliable and easier to develop.

NEW CHALLENGES

By the 1970s, Hamilton wanted new challenges. She wanted the technology she worked on at MIT to develop faster. And she wanted more people to use it. So she started her own company. In 1976, she launched Higher Order

Software (HOS) and ran the company. It built products that made her technology faster and easier to use. The US military used technology from HOS.

A NEW VISION

Hamilton left HOS in 1985. The next year, she founded Hamilton Technologies, Inc. (HTI), in Cambridge. She leads this company too. It developed the Universal Systems Language (USL). USL is a language for building systems and software. It is based on a math theory Hamilton developed. USL relies on **function maps (FMaps)**, or things to be done. It also has **type maps (TMaps)**, for types of objects. USL combines both kinds of maps. USL systems help avoid coding errors.

HTI also created the 001 Tool Suite. Companies can use this software to work with USL systems. Hamilton calls these products Development Before the Fact systems. In other words, Hamilton's software prevents problems before they occur.

RECOGNIZING A LEADER

By the mid-1980s, Hamilton had created a new model for developing systems and software. She discovered that most software engineer problems came from "fixing wrong things up." She knew they should "[do] things in the right way in the first place."

In 1986, the Association for Women in Computing gave Hamilton their Ada Lovelace Award. This award goes to women who make outstanding achievements in science and technology. It also goes to people whose work has helped other women in computer science. The award recognized Hamilton as a software pioneer.

Ada Lovelace is credited as the first person to write a computer program.

ADA LOVELACE

Ada Lovelace (1815–1852) is the world's first computer programmer. She was born in London, England. Her father—George Byron, or Lord Byron—was a famous poet. Her mother, Anne Isabella Milbanke, loved math.

Lovelace excelled at math too. In 1833, her tutor introduced her to Charles Babbage, a math professor. Babbage had an idea for a computing machine called the Analytical Engine. The machine would speed up math calculations. It would have memory and make choices. It would repeat instructions.

Lovelace understood how important the machine could be to technology. In 1843, Richard Taylor published a set of her notes about the engine. The notes included instructions for the machine. This was the world's first computer program. The Association for Women in Computing has given the Ada Lovelace Award to women achievers since the late 1970s.

Chapter 5

Skylab orbited Earth from 1973 to 1979.

"A PIONEERING EFFORT"

Hamilton had worked in computer science for many years. NASA gave her the Exceptional Space Act Award in 2003 to honor her work. "The Apollo flight software Ms. Hamilton and her team developed was truly a pioneering effort," said Sean O'Keefe of NASA.

A few years later, in 2009, Earlham College gave Hamilton an Outstanding Alumni Award. It described her as a pioneer in software engineering and in NASA space programs. Besides the Apollo missions, she also worked on Skylab, the first US space station.

ACTION FIGURE

Hamilton continues with her life's work. She wants to bring USL to more people around the world. She wants her software to be even better.

Maia Weinstock, an editor for *MIT News*, had an idea to honor Hamilton in a fun way. In 2016, Weinstock shared it with Lego. Her idea was to create a Lego set that included five NASA pioneers—all women. They are Margaret Hamilton, Katherine Johnson (a NASA researcher), Sally Ride (the first US woman in space), Nancy Grace Roman (an astronomer who helped plan the Hubble Space Telescope), and Mae Jemison (the first African American woman in space).

In November 2016, President Barack Obama announced that Hamilton would be honored with the Presidential Medal of Freedom. The medal is given to people who have made special contributions to the interests of the United States.

President Obama said Hamilton stood for all the women of her generation who helped send people into space.

Astronauts such as Mae Jemison rely on computer software to keep them alive in space.

SPEAKING TO THE FUTURE

The words *software engineering* had once been a joke. Now they describe a *multibillion*-dollar industry! Space exploration costs a lot of money. Hamilton knows that good software saves NASA money. And if a program does not cost too much, NASA is more likely to launch it.

The future of space exploration depends on more than just money. It depends on young people too. Hamilton says that studying literature, history, and STEM subjects are important for building careers. They are important for living life. So are creativity and problem solving. She points to team projects and playing games as good ways to have fun. They also help people learn to be open-minded and to get along with others. We still have much to learn about the universe. Hamilton hopes to keep exploring.

TECH TALK

"The concepts [Hamilton] and her team created became the building blocks for modern 'software engineering.'"

—NASA administrator Sean O'Keefe

TIMELINE

1936
Margaret Hamilton is born on August 17 in Paoli, Indiana.

1958
Hamilton graduates from Earlham College.

1959
Hamilton accepts a programming job at Massachusetts Institute of Technology (MIT).

1965
Hamilton becomes the director of the Software Engineering Division at MIT, which is working on NASA's Apollo missions.

1969
The Apollo 11 mission lands *Eagle* on the moon. Neil Armstrong and Buzz Aldrin are the first people to step onto the moon.

1976
Hamilton cofounds the Higher Order Software (HOS) company.

1986
Hamilton founds Hamilton Technologies, Inc. (HTI), in Cambridge, Massachusetts. She receives the Ada Lovelace Award for her scientific and technical work.

2003
Hamilton receives the NASA Exceptional Space Act Award for her work in science and technology.

2016
Maia Weinstock of *MIT News* proposes a Margaret Hamilton Lego figure. Hamilton is also honored with the Presidential Medal of Freedom.

SOURCE NOTES

6 "July 20, 1969: One Giant Leap for Mankind," NASA, July 14, 2014, https://www .nasa.gov/mission_pages/apollo/apollo11.html.

6 Lily Rotham, "Remembering the *Apollo 11* Moon Landing with the Woman Who Made It Happen," *Time*, July 20, 2015, http://time.com/3948364/moon-landing -apollo-11-margaret-hamilton.

9 Margaret Hamilton, "Margaret Hamilton's Introduction," transcript, Apollo Guidance Computer History Project, July 27, 2001, http://authors.library.caltech.edu/5456/1 /hrst.mit.edu/hrs/apollo/public/conference1/hamilton-intro.htm.

15 Robert McMillan, "Her Code Got Humans on the Moon—and Invented Software Itself," *Wired*, October 13, 2015, http://www.wired.com/2015/10/margaret -hamilton-nasa-apollo.

19 "Apollo 11 Mission Overview," NASA, accessed November 17, 2016, http://www .nasa.gov/mission_pages/apollo/missions/apollo11.html.

21 Margaret H. Hamilton and William R. Hackler, "Universal Systems Language for Preventative Systems Engineering," paper 40, Conference on Systems Engineering Research, Hoboken, NJ, March 14–16, 2007, http://www.htius.com.

24 "NASA Honors Apollo Engineer," NASA, September 3, 2003, https://www.hq .nasa.gov/alsj/a11/a11Hamilton.html.

28 Ibid.

GLOSSARY

function maps (FMaps)
USL maps that define the functions in a system and the relationships among them

programming
designing instructions that can be followed by a computer system

software engineer
a person who creates software (computer code) and follows a standard set of rules for making reliable software

type maps (TMaps)
USL maps of types of objects and the relationships among them

FURTHER INFORMATION

BOOKS

Ignotofsky, Rachel. *Women in Science: 50 Fearless Pioneers Who Changed the World*. New York: Ten Speed, 2016. Meet fifty amazing women scientists, including computer scientist Ada Lovelace.

McAneney, Caitie. *Women in Space*. New York: PowerKids, 2016. Learn about Sally Ride, Mae Jemison, Eileen Collins, and other women who have been to space.

Waxman, Laura Hamilton. *Computer Engineer Ruchi Sanghvi*. Minneapolis: Lerner Publications, 2015. Discover how another woman helped blaze her own trail in computer engineering.

WEBSITES

EngineerGirl
http://www.engineergirl.org
Meet real women engineers. Learn what they do. Find out about engineering clubs you can join. Take quizzes. You can even enter the yearly essay contest!

Great Minds: Margaret Hamilton
https://www.youtube.com/watch?v=PPLDZMjgaf8&index=2&list =PLC31BOC382F9585D6
Hank Green, a host on YouTube's *SciShow* series, talks about Margaret Hamilton's career. The video has lots of cool photos too.

NASA Kids' Club
http://www.nasa.gov/kidsclub/index.html
Play games, watch videos, and see cool photos at this site just for kids. Keep up on all the NASA missions to outer space to learn about Mars, Jupiter, Pluto, and more.

LERNER

SOURCE

Expand learning beyond the printed book. Download free, complementary educational resources for this book from our website, www.lerneresource.com.

INDEX

ABOUT THE AUTHOR

Domenica Di Piazza is an editorial director in nonfiction publishing. She also writes nonfiction books for young readers. She enjoys learning about science and scientists, traveling, and cooking, and she would one day love to visit the Large Hadron Collider near Geneva, Switzerland. She lives in Minneapolis with her spouse and their dog and three cats.